Original title:
Wildwood Wanderings

Copyright © 2025 Creative Arts Management OÜ
All rights reserved.

Author: Lila Davenport
ISBN HARDBACK: 978-1-80566-748-3
ISBN PAPERBACK: 978-1-80566-818-3

Lullabies of the Woodland Breeze

The owls hoot a silly tune,
The raccoons dance by the moon.
A squirrel tries to join the fun,
But trips over nuts, oh what a run!

The frogs croak in perfect rhyme,
While crickets click in their prime.
With every rustle, a giggle spreads,
As cheeky mice frolic in their beds.

The Spirit of the Emerald Labyrinth

In a maze of green, oh what a sight,
The hedgehogs are holding a wrestling fight.
A badger's snoring, snug in his den,
While the raccoons plan mischief again!

A fox with a flair, wearing a hat,
Recites odd poems to a sleepy cat.
The trees chuckle softly, their branches sway,
As the forest comes alive in a quirky way.

A Tapestry of Twisted Vines

Vines twist and turn, a dance of glee,
Tangled feet of a bumblebee.
A gopher sneezes, that's quite the sound,
And the startled birds scatter all around.

The butterflies giggle, flaunting their hues,
While a tortoise mulls over his shoes.
A party of critters, all cheery and bright,
Celebrate nature with pure delight.

Unraveling the Forest's Secrets

Whispers of laughter echo through trees,
As the squirrels plot tricks while swaying in the breeze.
A deer plays hide-and-seek with delight,
But gets caught in branches—what a sight!

The owls wink from their lofty dome,
While the chipmunks gather, feeling right at home.
Every nook hides a tale so grand,
In this silly world of nature's band.

Whispers Among the Pines

The pines gossip like old friends,
Sharing secrets in the breeze.
A squirrel sneezes, laughter blends,
As branches sway with perfect ease.

A raccoon dons a hat so bright,
He struts like he owns the place.
The owls hoot, a playful fright,
While chipmunks scamper with their grace.

Woodpeckers drum a silly tune,
As if the trees join in the fun.
A fox prances under the moon,
Sprinkling mischief on the run.

Among the trunks, a dance unfolds,
Nature's comedy, pure delight.
With whispers shared and stories told,
The forest laughs, all through the night.

Secrets of the Forest Floor

Beneath the ferns, the creatures play,
Where ladybugs host a tea.
A caterpillar shimmies away,
In a waltz with a bumblebee.

Mushrooms sprout with funny hats,
Winking at the strolling deer.
A groundhog giggles at the chats,
As rabbits dive into their beer.

The roots all twist in silly ways,
Giggling through the dirt and grime.
A fox tells tales of crazy days,
While lizards soak up sunny time.

Secrets buried near the roots,
In laughter's echo, life abounds.
The forest floor, where nature hoots,
In harmony, with funny sounds.

Echoes of Untamed Paths

Along the trail, the squirrels race,
Chasing shadows in a reel.
A rabbit's hop, a funny face,
Leaves everyone with a wheel.

The path twists round with silly signs,
"Beware of wandering weeds!"
Where patches bloom like playful vines,
And every step, a joke exceeds.

At every bend, a chuckle waits,
A porcupine with quite the stew.
The wind plays tunes of glorious fates,
While leaves applaud their leafy crew.

Echoes bounce from tree to tree,
An orchestra of nature's glee.
With laughter lighting up the way,
Adventure beckons, come what may.

Beneath the Canopy's Embrace

Beneath the canopy, life's a jest,
With shadows dancing, twirling fine.
A turtle boasts he's better dressed,
And steals the show, all align.

A parrot jokes, the branches sway,
"Why did the tree drop its leaves?"
The answer hides in leaf-strewn play,
While laughter rings, the forest weaves.

Beneath the boughs, oh what a sight,
A party thrown by birds so spry.
They chirp and sing 'til the night,
As stars peek through the darkened sky.

In nature's arms, the fun is grand,
With giggles echoing through the land.
A celebration, wild and bright,
As creatures dance in pure delight.

Dreaming Under the Canopy

In the shade of huge green leaves,
Silly squirrels dance in a tease.
A rabbit leaps with a comic flair,
While sleepy bees buzz without a care.

Raccoons roll with a giggling sound,
Chasing shadows all around.
A deer trips over a fallen limb,
And all the forest joins in a whim.

Into the Heart of the Tamarack

I wandered deep where the trees play,
Chasing shadows 'til the end of day.
A moose slipped past in oversized shoes,
Winking at me with amused views.

Chipmunks chatter, quite the loud crew,
While sticky sap gets caught in my shoe.
I giggle at ducks with their own parade,
As they paddle on by, unafraid.

Reflections of a Stream's Serenade

The stream hums tunes of splashes bright,
Frogs join in, what a marvelous sight!
Dragonflies dance with a flair so bold,
As water glistens in shades of gold.

Fish flip-flop with a giggle and splash,
While turtles sunbathe, oh what a clash!
I stomp in, water sprays high above,
Who knew the woods would tickle with love?

Mystic Paths of the Silent Glade

Through a glade where silence reigns,
A squirrel sings of his wild complaints.
A wind whispers jokes through branches wide,
While chipmunks snicker as they slide.

The mushrooms chuckle, all lined in rows,
Trying to hide from the snuffling nose.
A fox in a cloak of orange flair,
Cracks a grin, too clever to share.

Musing by the Glittering brook

By a brook that sparkles bright,
A frog croaks in the moonlight.
He's trying out his opera tune,
But all we hear is quite a toom!

A fish jumps up with a splash,
Says, "Frog, your notes are quite brash!"
Together they create a scene,
A nature show, both loud and keen.

The water's edge holds little charms,
A duck quacks loud, then flails its arms.
It splashes, dives, and makes quite mess,
Oh, what joy in this playful jest!

As I sit with leaf and bough,
I can't help but raise a brow.
The woodland's full of silly sights,
Where laughter dances 'neath the lights.

The Poetry of the Untamed

In the tangled underbrush,
A squirrel scribbles, none can hush.
It writes of acorns, dreams so grand,
And hides its notes in the soft sand.

A badger reads with gentle pride,
Says, "Keep it secret, never hide."
But then a rabbit hops on by,
It snags the poem, oh my, oh my!

The forest hums with rhythms weird,
As trees toss words for all to be steered.
The wind whispers tales, some funny,
Of how the sun once asked for honey.

Beneath the boughs, the laughter swells,
Where all the critters share their spells.
In this wild, free, poetic play,
Nature's humor brightens the day.

Glimmers in the Foliage

Through dapples of light we wander,
Sunbeams play, oh don't you ponder?
A chipmunk scurries, grains in cheek,
Looks like he's hiding from some streak!

In leafy greens, a shadow flits,
A deer leaps by, doing wild skits.
It trips on roots, tumbles and rolls,
Who knew such grace could have such holes?

The flowers giggle in a breeze,
They dance about with such great ease.
A bee buzzes in with a boast,
"Be careful of my honey toast!"

Every rustle brings a smile,
Nature's quirks stretch on for a while.
With sparkles here and laughter there,
The woodland sings a fun affair.

Reveries of the Woodland Spirits

Amidst the trees, the spirits play,
They twirl and twist, and dance all day.
One trips on roots, falls with a sigh,
"Watch where you sprout!" another sly.

A whisper floats on gentle breeze,
"Who stole my hat?" says one with ease.
Laughter echoes through each glen,
"Not again! That's your third time, friend!"

They poke their heads from mossy nooks,
And gather tales like cherished books.
A spider weaves stories so fine,
With each fine thread, it starts to shine.

In the twilight's glow, fun unfurls,
The woodland sways, it twirled, it twirls.
In mischievous glee, they take their part,
Whispering magic with a laughing heart.

Shadows of Ancient Oak

Beneath the boughs so wide and grand,
I tripped on roots, oh did I stand!
A squirrel laughed, it took my hat,
He chattered loud, 'You clumsy brat!'

The shadows danced, a teasing game,
As I pursued that furry flame.
With twiggy legs and haste I dashed,
Through branches low, my patience crashed!

Each leaf confided, 'What a jest!'
As I just yearned for a quiet rest.
But here I find, in nature's fray,
The playfulness of a bright green day.

Footprints in the Underbrush

Oh look, a track, perhaps a deer,
Or something else that brought me cheer.
But wait! What's this, a clumsy sign?
A trail of cookies, half divine!

I followed crumbs like Hansel's quest,
But found a badger taking rest.
He shook his head, 'Not snack for you!'
'But I just wanted a nibble too!'

Through thorny paths and leafy traps,
I chased the critters, took some laps.
Each footprint led me round and round,
A merry chase with mischief found!

Embracing the Mossy Twilight

In twilight's grasp, where shadows blend,
I bumped a bush, my trusty friend.
With laughter loud, the stars came out,
And moss said, 'Dare you dance about?'

The fireflies blinked, a disco scene,
While I just tried to stay unseen.
But tripped on roots, oh what a sight!
The trees just chuckled, pure delight!

I spun in circles 'neath the sky,
The owls looked down with a big sigh.
'In moss we trust, just let it be!'
The thrumming beat of trees in glee.

Songs of the Wandering Breeze

A breeze blew in, just like a tease,
It whispered softly through the trees.
I tried to catch it, what a laugh,
It danced away, an airy calf!

Around the glades, it swirled and twirled,
My hat flew off, my senses whirled.
With every gust, a giggle stole,
And nature played its funny role!

A leap, a hop, through grassy lanes,
The breeze and I became best friends.
Together we caused quite a stir,
In every nook, a secret whir!

The Call of the Forgotten Trails

In the woods, where shadows creep,
A squirrel's chatter turns to sheep.
A chipmunk fumbles, trying to hide,
As I trip over roots with pride.

The trees giggle, their branches sway,
A mischievous breeze leads me astray.
A wanderer's charm, I can't resist,
Nature's laughter in the mist.

Dappled Sunlight on Fern-Covered Stones

Sunbeams peek through leaves so green,
Tickling the ferns, a playful scene.
A bug-eyed toad breaks into a dance,
While I attempt a forest prance!

Stones glisten like jewels in a crown,
I wave to the fox who wears a frown.
A gentle nudge from a twig in flight,
Turns my stumble into pure delight.

Journey Through the Sylvan Dream

A path so crooked, I lose my shoe,
The owls hoot, must think it's new.
I follow a trail of fallen leaves,
Where laughter echoes, and mischief weaves.

A rabbit pops up, nose twitching fast,
As I sip berries, which won't last.
The forest dances, a playful scheme,
In this whimsical sylvan dream.

Where the Foxgloves Danced

In fields of flowers, colors collide,
The bees are buzzing, full of pride.
While I twirl, the petals swirl,
A clumsy ballet in a floral whirl.

The foxgloves giggle, their petals sway,
Inviting me in for a wild play.
A tumble and roll, the dance is grand,
Nature's jesters, take my hand!

The Dance of the Wandering Stream

A brook bows down with a bubbly cheer,
It splashes away each time we near.
The fish shake fins, and giggle too,
As frogs croak tunes for a waltzing crew.

With stones that skip like a child's laugh,
And reeds that sway in a silly half,
The turtle glides, wearing shades of green,
On water's stage, he's the dancing queen!

A log rolls past, in a grand ballet,
While dragonflies prance, in a flirty way.
Each ripple forms a comedy act,
Nature's humor is a vital fact.

But watch your step, heed the stream's own rhyme,
Or you may trip, and it won't be sublime.
With giggles echoing through the glade,
The stream invites you, come join its parade!

In Search of Forgotten Glades

I wandered off, with a map quite shifty,
In search of glades, the land seemed zifty.
The trees are tall, they laugh and tease,
While squirrels plot their nutty degrees.

The paths twist round like a riddle's bend,
Each turn reveals a new furry friend.
I asked a rabbit, where's that lost place?
He winked and hopped with a droll little grace.

A signpost groaned, "You're going the wrong way!"
But it spoke in riddles, oh what a display!
I tripped on roots, but the trees all giggled,
Their whispers carried the fun that mingled.

Finally found, a glade so sweet,
Where sunbeams dance on a mossy seat.
The foliage chuckles, all around me,
In these hidden lands, joy roams free!

Guardians of the Grove

The old oak stands with an owl's big stare,
"Why are you here?" it asks in the air.
A squirrel replied, "To party, you see!"
The tree shook its branches, "Well, just wait for me!"

With hedgehogs wearing tiny hats of grass,
They twirled and twirled with a giggling sass.
The guardians of lore, they join in the fun,
As fireflies burst forth, each lighting a run.

The wise old tree shared tales of the past,
Of mischief and magic, too wild to last.
The rabbits jumped high, in choreographed leaps,
While crickets crooned soft, to the rhythm that creeps.

So if you wander, and hear giggles soar,
Remember the grove is a dance floor galore.
With guardians smiling, and joy all around,
Each visit's a treasure, where laughter abounds!

Petals in the Wind

A breeze swept by with a chuckle and cheer,
Carrying petals, like confetti near.
They twirled and spun, in a carefree waltz,
Each flower child giggling, without a fault.

A bumblebee buzzed in a ticklish chase,
Chasing the petals, in a dizzying race.
The daisies laughed as they waved their heads,
"Come dance with us, forget your dreads!"

A dandelion puffed with a grand flair,
"Let's scatter wishes and fluff through the air!"
With each little seed that flew from its crown,
A wish for pure joy, in a swirling gown.

So join the flutter, be part of the spree,
In a faded field, where we all run free.
For petals in the wind, hold laughter and play,
A whimsical journey, in every sway!

Flight of the Feathered Wanderer

A bird in the sky, what a sight to see,
Chasing his tail, he laughs with glee.
With a dive and a twist, he makes quite a scene,
A feathered acrobat, the forest's clown routine.

He perched on a branch, but missed his mark,
Landed in a bush, oh what a lark!
He shakes off the leaves, and gives a loud tweet,
A comedy show, where birds never retreat.

With his winged friends, they gather for fun,
Playing tag through the trees, oh what a run!
Their squawks echo loudly, a raucous delight,
In their feathery frolic, from morning till night.

The Breath of the Breezes

The breezes blow in, with whispers of cheer,
Tickling my nose, as they suddenly appear.
They dance through the branches, so playful and spry,
A jolly uprising, that lifts spirits high.

One gust came rushing, it stole my hat,
I ran after it, and nearly fell flat!
It swirled round a tree, and then off it went,
With a chuckling swish, oh what a torment!

The breeze teased the flowers, made them sway side to side,
Spinning petals like dancers, with nothing to hide.
Their laughter accompanied, on this joyous beat,
In the game of the wind, no one admits defeat.

In the Presence of Elder Trees

The old trees stood tall, with a grin in their bark,
Whispering secrets, holding a spark.
They leaned in to gossip, in a creaky old tone,
"Did you hear what the squirrels did? Oh, what a groan!"

A gathering of branches, like arms spread wide,
They tell the best tales, with laughter inside.
"Remember the time, a hawk tried to sneak,
But slipped on a branch? Oh, that was unique!"

With roots intertwined, they shared silly jests,
While critters below joined in for the quests.
A festival of laughs, in the shade they bestow,
In the company of giants, it's a hoot, not a woe.

Tread Softly on the Forest Floor

With each step I take, the leaves give a crunch,
A symphony of sounds, that makes raccoons lunch!
The critters look up, with wide, startled eyes,
"What's that noise?" they mutter, in disbelief sighs.

The twigs snap like popcorn, beneath my two feet,
While squirrels chitter loudly, retreating in beat.
"Who's tramping around?" they say with a frown,
This clumsy giant is wearing them down!

I laugh at the chaos, my shoes are a mess,
Nature's comedy scene, oh what a jest!
As I tiptoe along, I try to restore,
A soft-footed promise, to tread just once more.

Beneath the Arching Branches

Beneath the arching branches, I tripped on a vine,
My shoes flew off, oh what a sign!
A squirrel laughed from its lofty seat,
"Where's the fashion in bare feet?"

A hedgehog rolled by, quite proud of his quills,
Claiming he's king of the woodland thrills.
I asked him for tips, he just rolled away,
"Style comes with spikes, that's my way!"

The wobbly path got sneaky and sly,
I stumbled and tumbled, oh me, oh my!
A rabbit snickered, "Don't hurry, my friend!"
"Nature's all about the fun that you spend!"

The sun began setting, the shadows all played,
I danced with the trees, in my clumsy parade.
With laughter and mishaps, I bid the day bye,
"Come back tomorrow, we'll see if I fly!"

Enchanted Echoes of the Pines

In the whisper of pines, I took a big swing,
And knocked over a bee, oh dear, that's the thing!
The buzzing brigade chased me all around,
"Next time! Watch your step on this magical ground!"

A deer peeked out, with a wink and a grin,
"Is that laughter I hear, or the buzz of a win?"
I couldn't decide; I'd laugh and I'd pout,
For what's more enchanting than fun all about?

With flowers a-dancing, I thought I'd join in,
But alas, tripped on something, it must be my chin!
The daisies all giggled, I joined in their laugh,
"Let's bloom where we're planted, and dance in the grass!"

Through echoes of joy, we spun 'round and 'round,
In the charming embrace of this forest confound.
Together we chuckled till day turned to night,
In enchanted woods, everything felt just right!

The Enigma of the Twilit Trail

On the twilit trail where shadows grow wide,
I met a lost gnome with five hats piled high.
He scratched his head, all puzzled and spry,
"Is it hat weather or is that just a lie?"

The bats overhead seemed to flap with glee,
As I miscounted my steps, one, two, now three!
A frog croaked loudly, "You're off and you're wrong,
But it's great to see you! Come sing us a song!"

Twilight giggles bounced off the barky brigade,
With critters all dancing, I tried to invade!
"I'm not so sure I can follow your lead,"
A wise old owl hooted, "Just fly, take your heed!"

So I skipped and I hopped with friends by my side,
On this puzzly trail that we hilariously ride.
With laughter as our compass, we'll wander til dawn,
In the mystery of dusk, our joy carried on!

The Song of the Woodlands

In the woodlands I stumbled, on branches so low,
The birds all erupted, "Oh watch where you go!"
With a flap and a flurry, they cheered from the leaves,
"I'd trip too, if I wore these two left-footed sleeves!"

A raccoon then joined with a laugh that was grand,
"Let's sing with the trees, won't you take my hand?"
I grabbed at the air with my clumsy ballet,
"Follow my lead!" But I fell, to his play!

A chorus of critters rang out with delight,
As I rolled in the moss, what a wonderful sight!
The melody swirled, right through branches and bark,
We sang as we tumbled, till the skies turned dark.

So here's to the song that the woodland will share,
With mishaps and giggles, we dance without care.
Each critter a note, in this symphony wild,
Nature's own laughter, a sweet, joyful child!

Moonlit Secrets of the Glen

In glimmers bright, the critters dance,
A raccoon twirls, his pants askew,
The owl hoots loud, gives quite a glance,
While shadows waltz beneath the dew.

A sly fox grins, with mischief rife,
He's swiped the cheese from that picnic spread,
The laughter weaves a tale of life,
As all the forest joins the thread.

With moonlit giggles, trees confide,
Each rustle tells a secret joke,
A squirrel struts with nuts in pride,
While branches sway, the night awoke.

The fireflies wink, they tease and flit,
A chorus sings of joy and play,
In this odd glen, not one does sit,
With silly hearts, we laugh away.

Ramble Through Rustic Realms

With muddy boots, we stomp and slide,
We chase a breeze, we trip and fall,
An ant parade, they strut with pride,
While we just giggle at it all.

A cow wears shades, so cool and sly,
She seems to know the farmer's rules,
While rabbits leap and swat the sky,
They mock our clumsiness like fools.

The trees gossip in whispers low,
About the shenanigans we plot,
Each winding path, a tale to show,
Of garden gnomes who've lost the lot.

As twilight paints the fields with gold,
We find a laugh in every nook,
Our tales of mischief, fun retold,
In rustic realms, we're hooks and cooks.

The Enchanted Boughs' Ballet

Where branches dip and twirl around,
   A squirrel pirouettes with flair,
The wind conducts its playful sound,
   As butterflies flit without a care.

A hedgehog joins in on the beat,
   With tiny steps that shine so bright,
A concert hall amid the wheat,
   As twinkling stars laugh in the night.

Nestled in bushes, frogs recite,
   Their croaks like songs from ages past,
Each bough a dancer in the light,
   In nature's ball, we find our cast.

As laughter echoes with the breeze,
   The forest glows with mischief's glee,
In this grand show, no one can tease,
   For all are welcome, wild and free.

Surprises Beneath the Boughs

Beneath the leaves, a gnome snores loud,
His hat askew, the mushrooms grow,
While chipmunks stage a circus crowd,
With acorns tossed in every row.

A snail in glasses takes a peek,
At all the antics on display,
While hedgehogs plan a prank this week,
We giggle at their clever ways.

Each rustle hides a funny tale,
From whispered winds to dancing bees,
A waltz of nature, quick and frail,
Our joy spills forth like honeyed breeze.

So come and join this merry show,
Where thrumming hearts find sweet surprise,
In playful woods, let laughter flow,
As dreams take flight beneath the skies.

Pathways Through the Verdant Veil

In the woods, I lost my shoe,
Chasing squirrels, what a view!
Bouncing branches, birds that sing,
Who knew trees could do gymnastics thing?

A raccoon waved, it stole my map,
I followed it, oh what a trap!
Found a clearing, thought I'd rest,
Sat on mushrooms, that was my test.

Ferns danced wildly, caught in a breeze,
I tripped on roots, oh, if you please!
Laughed with flowers, such silly sights,
Told a joke to passing lights.

Hopping rabbits joined in my spree,
"Hey, come here, have a cup of tea!"
Nature teems with giggling sounds,
In this maze, joy abounds!

Nature's Hidden Labyrinth

Just a stroll turned to a race,
I followed trails, lost all my grace.
A fox popped up, gave me a wink,
"Care for a snack? Or maybe a drink?"

Bark on trees, like riddles to crack,
Who knew nature had all this knack?
I pondered hard, what could it mean?
A moose appeared, said, "Get clean!"

I wandered far, with ants as my guide,
They pointed left, yet I went right.
Ran into mushrooms doing ballet,
They laughed, and said, "Join the fray!"

Caught in a bush, like a comical play,
I wriggled and jigged, in my own way.
So many paths, with adventure in store,
Nature's humor, oh how I adore!

The Language of Leaf and Bark

Whispers rustle through the green,
"Did you hear what the willow seen?"
Oak giggled, shared a tall tale,
While pine needles danced without fail.

Every leaf has jokes to share,
"Stop and listen, if you dare!"
Sassy petals, blooming bright,
"Tell me more, is it day or night?"

Nature speaks in funny puns,
Barking trees, they love to run.
I told a joke to a nearby rock,
It chuckled back, quite a shock!

Gathered friends, a quirky crew,
Had a blast at morning dew.
In this wild chat, we surely thrive,
With chuckles and giggles, we feel alive!

Murmurs in the Mossy Glade

In a glade with moss so deep,
I heard a critter softly peep.
Turned to find it, bold and spry,
A snail with shades, oh my, oh my!

"Slow down!" it said, "Why in such haste?
The woods are full of things to taste!"
So we sat, shared stories galore,
Of acorns, trees, and things we adore.

Funny fungi joined the fun,
With jokes that sparkled in the sun.
They giggled quite loud, made quite a scene,
With mushroom caps and laughs unseen.

We had a ball, in this lush parade,
Dancing with shadows that never fade.
In the glade, where mischief unfolds,
Nature's laughter is pure as gold!

The Language of Leaf and Bark

In the forest, trees start to chat,
Squirrels laugh, while a deer tips his hat.
Bark to bark, they share silly tales,
Of a raccoon who plans to steal some snails.

Grasshoppers hop with a jolly tune,
While frogs croak loudly, dreaming of June.
The sun creeps in, the woodpecker knocks,
They giggle at squirrels storing their socks.

A chipmunk writes poems on roots so old,
About nuts in a dance, all shiny and gold.
With whispers of leaves, they all agree,
A nutty good time in their leafy spree.

Mushrooms giggle under the brightening sun,
With mushrooms wearing hats, oh what fun!
The language of leaves, a jolly affair,
In the forest, they dance without a care.

Fables From the Thicket

In thickets thick, tales do unfold,
Of a beetle who claimed he was bold.
He challenged a snail to a race one day,
But ended up stuck in a puddle of clay.

A wise old owl said, 'Never rush!',
As a hare tripped over a bush's lush brush.
The turtle grinned, moving slow as a dream,
While the hare thought he'd win — or so it would seem.

Berries gossip high in the sky,
As bees buzz by with a sweet little sigh.
Worms wag their tails with fables to share,
Of a crow who thought he could rock a bright flare.

Each creature laughs at the folly around,
In a world where surprises abound.
In the thicket, they gather, ready to play,
Creating their tales, come join the ballet!

The Maze of Whispering Willows

In a maze of willows, secrets do blend,
Whispers of frogs who call each other friend.
A lost little bunny with big floppy ears,
Seeks the right path through laughter and cheers.

The willows sway gently, sharing a jest,
Of a fox who thought he was simply the best.
He tripped over roots, fell flat on his back,
Leaving the hedgehogs in stitches, oh, what a crack!

Caterpillars wiggle and dance on the breeze,
While squirrels perform acrobatics with ease.
In the maze, every twist brings a grin,
And the laughter of pixies chimes in with a spin.

Lost in the shadows, a party takes flight,
As the moon peeks in, delivering light.
The willows keep secrets, but laughter shines through,
In the maze, boundless joy, just waiting for you!

Adventures in the Hidden Grove

In a hidden grove where the giggles abound,
A hedgehog declares he's the fastest around.
But racing a turtle at one sunny dawn,
He learned that slow wins, while fast can be gone.

Frogs in a chorus sing 'ribbit-ribbit',
While fireflies dance, oh, what a snippet!
A raccoon with mischief is up to some tricks,
Hiding his snacks in a pile of old sticks.

Under the shrubs, where secrets reside,
A party of critters seek joy, not to hide.
With laughter so loud, it echoes through trees,
They celebrate friendship with giggles and ease.

Adventures unfold, like tales in the air,
In the hidden grove, where all truly care.
Each moment a treasure, each laugh a delight,
In this woodland playhouse, everything's bright!

Mosaic of Nature's Colors

In the forest where moss grows bright,
A squirrel plays hide-and-seek with light.
He tripped on a root, oh what a show,
Then danced with the leaves, a comical flow.

A flower sneezed, its petals all shook,
The trees whispered tales from an old storybook.
A butterfly giggled, flapping its wings,
While ants in a row strutted like kings.

Bright berries chuckled, full of delight,
A raccoon rolled by, what an odd sight!
The colors all mingled, a vibrant mess,
In this comedy act of nature's dress.

As day turned to dusk, shadows took flight,
With critters all winding down for the night.
Yet laughter echoed in the twilight glow,
For in this wild place, fun forever will grow.

Starlit Nights in the Thicket

Beneath the stars where the owls reside,
A hedgehog stumbled, with pride as his guide.
He rolled down the hill, what a goofy sight,
Bumped into a bush, and gave a small fright.

The fireflies twinkled, a sparkling cheer,
While frogs croaked tunes, all music we hear.
A rabbit wore glasses, quite hip for the night,
Critiques of his style sparked a fun light.

As crickets played fiddles, the nighthawks swooped,
The moon chuckled softly, while shadows looped.
An owl made a pun, a wise guy no doubt,
And laughter erupted, a hoot without doubt.

In the thicket of joy, where silliness leads,
Nature's own revelers, fulfilling their needs.
Under the blanket of night, all aglow,
We dance with the stars, oh what a show!

The Spirit of the Overgrown Path

On a path overgrown where the wild tangles,
A snail took a joyride, oh how it wrangles.
With laughter of mice echoing close,
He wondered aloud if he'd floated like a ghost.

A hedgehog in sunglasses, so chic and so cool,
Strolled with a swagger, breaking the rule.
A dandelion giggled, tickled by breeze,
While the stones murmured jokes, aiming to please.

In the shade of the trees, laughter danced wide,
As geese wore top hats and paraded with pride.
The wildflowers swayed, their petals a-flutter,
While the air was filled with giggles and clutter.

On this unruly path, where silliness reigns,
Nature's humor flows through the branches like veins.
With each step or tumble, a laugh we will find,
In the spirit of play, we're all intertwined.

Skirmishes of the Evening Wind

As the evening breeze took a playful sweep,
It tussled with branches, a ruckus to keep.
A leaf zoomed by, with a giggling sound,
Spinning in circles, then tumbling down.

The wind whispered secrets to butterflies bold,
Who stumbled and fumbled, all laughter uncontrolled.
A grasshopper leapt, trying hard to impress,
But landed in mud—a comical mess!

Then came along a mischievous pine,
Swaying and chuckling, a fun little sign.
With each twist and turn, a secret it told,
Of friendships and laughter, worth more than gold.

In the heart of the woods, where giggles don't end,
The evening wind brings both chaos and friends.
Through tickles of air, and dances so wild,
Nature's comedy plays on, oh how it's styled!

Revelations of the Woodland Muse

In shady glades, a squirrel spoke,
"I'd trade my nuts for a funny joke!"
The trees all giggled, leaves did sway,
As shadows danced, and critters played.

The wise old owl took off his specs,
And whispered tales of forest hexes.
"Watch your step, or you might trip,
On mushrooms sprouting from a ship!"

Bright fireflies flickered, brought their light,
While rabbits held a ball each night.
With moonlit laughter, hearts ran wild,
In nature's realm, the dreamer's child.

So come partake in this woodland jest,
For every leaf here knows the best!
Of joy and laughter, soft and bold,
The forest's secrets all retold!

Soft Murmurs of the Thicket

In thickets deep, a rabbit trod,
With carrots tucked, he gave a nod.
"Do you see the mushrooms, all in rows?"
He whispered softly, where the humor flows.

A hedgehog rolled with laughter loud,
"You'll never catch me in this crowd!"
The bushes rustled, secrets spilled,
Of playful games that nature thrilled.

The crickets chirped their nightly tune,
To serenade the sleepy moon.
A porcupine joined in with glee,
Singing off-key, yet fancy-free.

With soft murmurs under starlit skies,
The forest chuckled, surprise in eyes.
In each hidden nook, a laugh takes flight,
Where thicket tales spark pure delight!

Tales Carried by the Wind

From treetop heights, the wind did sigh,
With whispers low and hearts so spry.
"Did you hear that? The pine trees laugh!"
They buzzed with stories of a sweet giraffe.

With dandelions, they took to flight,
Sharing secrets, shadows, and light.
A woodpecker knocked, a beat divine,
While grasshoppers pranced, oh what a line!

"Hold tight your hats!" the breeze proclaimed,
"Or risk a hairdo wild and unclaimed!"
As leaves swirled round, they caught a jest,
In every gust, a serendipitous quest.

So listen close to what they share,
For every rustle holds a rare flair.
With laughter tossed like scattered seeds,
The wind's own tales fulfill our needs!

The Forest's Heartbeat

Underneath a towering pine,
The forest chuckled, oh so fine.
"Why did the squirrel cross the way?"
"To find his nuts – it's nutty play!"

The creek joined in with splashes sweet,
As frogs in chorus kept the beat.
With lily pads as their grand stage,
They leapt and danced like woodland sage.

A bear once tried his hand at jokes,
But stumbled on his own big hoax.
"I can't tell if I'm funny or just bear-y!"
The trees gave sighs, their roots grew weary.

With every thump, a mirthful thud,
The forest's heartbeat shook the mud.
In laughter's pulse, we find our way,
Through nature's charm, we joyfully play!

Dance of the Wildflowers

In fields of green, they swayed with glee,
A troupe of blooms, all wild and free.
They twirled and spun, in sunlight's glow,
With roots in dirt, they put on a show.

A daisy tripped on a rogue green stem,
Laid flat, it laughed, 'Well, who needs them?'
The buttercups giggled, in shades so bright,
Swaying together, what a silly sight!

The poppies puffed, had quite the flair,
In breezy waltz, they floated in air.
They whispered jokes to a passing bee,
"Catch us if you can, you won't get free!"

So if you stroll, in nature's embrace,
Watch wildflowers dance, in their joyful race.
Join them in laughter, lose all your cares,
For in playful blooms, life's laughter glares.

Enigma of the Hidden Thicket

In a thicket dense, where secrets hide,
A squirrel debates, with eyes open wide.
"Is acorn my treasure or just a façade?
How do I know if my nut's a dud?"

A rabbit with style, wears a fine coat,
Gambles with leaves, just to gloat.
While hedgehogs chuckle, all rolled up tight,
"Do we look fat, or is that just light?"

There's a mystery there, in shadows unseen,
A wise old owl with a tomfool grin.
"Who, me? I hoot! I'm so in the know!
Play peekaboo, and I'll steal the show!"

The thicket was buzzing, a comical place,
Where critters convened for a wild game of chase.
So join the riddle, unmask the cheer,
For life in the thicket is fun, that's clear!

Beneath the Whispering Boughs

Beneath the boughs, a rabbit pranced,
In whimsy's grip, his lunch he danced.
"Hey, Mr. Carrot, don't you run!
Together we'll hop, now wouldn't that be fun?"

A raccoon appeared, with a mask of cheer,
"Hide your snacks, friends! The bandits are here!"
With twinkling eyes, and a snicker so sly,
He pilfered some treats, then waved goodbye.

The birds above, in harmonized clucks,
Sang silly tunes about unlucky ducks.
While shadows flitted, and giggles would grow,
As trees whispered tales of old, to and fro.

Under the boughs, where laughter does bloom,
A merry gathering, dispelling the gloom.
So tiptoe, tiptoe, and listen, oh yes,
For beneath whispering boughs, there's comical zest!

The Solace of Solitary Strolls

In solitude's peace, I wander alone,
Chatting with squirrels, and feeling homegrown.
"Hey there, nutty! What's your latest joke?"
"I forgot again, I'm such a bloke!"

The path is my canvas, with twists and spins,
I mimic the pause of a skink with grins.
"Watch me, dear ferns, as I daintily prance!
Step lightly in leaves—that's my new dance!"

With every heartbeat, I hiccup with glee,
The echo of laughter surrounds even me.
"Is that a good tune, or perhaps a bee's buzz?
Let's throw a party for critters, because!"

Alone in the woods, it's a whimsical scene,
Where even the trees join the giggly routine.
So stroll, my friend, with a smile that swells,
For solace is best, where the laughter dwells!

www.ingramcontent.com/pod-product-compliance
Lightning Source LLC
Chambersburg PA
CBHW071812160426
43209CB00003B/61